DRAUGHTSMAN CIVIL FIRST YEAR MCQ

OBJECTIVE QUESTION ANSWERS

MANOJ DOLE

Digitization is the need of the time. In the future, training in industrial training institutes will need to be conducted using online internet to make training more convenient and easy. E-books containing a set of MCQ questions will be made available to the trainees as they need to be more accustomed to the multiple choice questions MCQ to prepare for the online exams taking place in their industrial training institutes.

With all these factors in mind, Mr. Manoj Madhukar Dole Instructor, Industrial Training Institute, Satara, has written books according to the new annual system and NSQF-5 syllabus. And they've created theoretical mobile apps and blogs to make training easier, and made all these educational materials available for download on the world famous websites Google Play Store, Amazon and Apple Book Store.

The books were published by Hon'ble Joint Director Shri Rajendra Ghume Saheb Regional Office of Vocational Education and Training, Pune on 9/1/2019, at this time Shri Prakash Saigavkar Saheb Principal Government Industrial Training Institute Aundh Pune, Shri Tukaram Misal Saheb Principal Govt. Q. Sanstha Satara, Shri Sachin Dhumal Saheb District Vocational Education and Training Officer Satara, Shri Yatin Pargaonkar Saheb Principal Govt. Q. Sanstha Kolhapur, Shri Vikas Teke Saheb Inspector Vocational Education and Training Regional Office Pune, Palekar Foods Products Pvt. Ltd. Entrepreneurial Chairman of Satara Mr. Nilkanthrao Palekar Saheb, Chairman of Hira Foods Mr. Ibrahim Baba Tamboli Saheb, Mrs. Shalmali Pawar Headmaster Government Technical School Center Satara and other dignitaries were present on the occasion.

Contents

Prologue

Draughtsman Civil First Year MCQ is a simple e-Book for ITI Engineering Course Draughtsman Civil, Revised NSQF Syllabus in 2022, Draughtsman Civil. It contains objective questions with underlined & bold correct answers MCQ covering all topics including all about the latest & Important about basic drawing (consisting geometrical figure, symbols & representations). Later the drawing skills imparted are drawing of different scales, projections, drawing of shoring, scaffolding, stone and brick masonry, foundation, damp proofing, arches / lintel etc. and observation of all safety aspects is mandatory. The safety aspects covers components like OSH&E, PPE, Fire extinguisher, First Aid and in addition 5S being taught. Different site survey (using Chain & tape, Prismatic compass, Plane table, Levelling instrument, Theodolite), field book entry, plotting, mapping, calculation of area, Drawing of carpentry joints and Electrical wiring, drawing of floors, slabs, vertical movements (viz.stair, lift well, ramp and escalator), drawing of different types of roof truss are being taught in the practical. and lots more.

We add new question answers with each new version. Please email us in case of any errors/omissions. This is arguably the largest and best e-Book for All engineering multiple choice questions and answers.

As a student you can use it for your exam prep. This e-Book is also useful for professors to refresh material.

Foreword

Vocational education and training is imparted through the Department of Vocational Education and Training through the Department of Business Education and Business Practical to supply multi-skilled artisans in line with the rapidly growing demand in the industrial sector in the 21st century. All the occupations within the institutions are important, as the trainees from these occupations develop multi-skills as per the demands of the industry.

with the noble intention of making available MCQ e-books suitable for all businesses, considering that all the examinations in all the industries in the industrial sector are conducted online and include MCQ method questions. Mr. Manoj Madhukar Dole has written a very good e-book on MCQ method as per the new annual syllabus. This e-book will definitely be a guide for all the trainees, trainee candidates, training instructors and others concerned.

The author of the book is Mr. Manoj Madhukar Dole, Instructor Gov. ITI Satara has 17 years of training experience. Written as a new annual pattern, this e-book incorporates modern digital QR Code technology to understand the layout, simple language, and simple syntax, diagrams and videos for each subject. So I am sure that this e-book will definitely be useful for in-depth study and exam practice. The work they have done is certainly commendable.

Mr. Tukaram Misal
Principal Government Industrial Training Institute Satara.

Preface

DGET New Delhi and CSTARI Kolkata have been implementing an annual pattern for all businesses in ITI since the August 2018 session. The examination system will also be changed and it will be online from this year and since all the questions are of Objective Type (MCQ), the trainees are in dire need of in-depth study. It is with this in mind that we are delighted to present the books based on the old NIMI pattern and a complete overview of the new annual pattern, and we hope that these books will be a guide for all business directors and trainees. Is.

For writing these books, Johar Awate Saheb, Principal of ITI Akluj. Former Principal of ITI Satara Saigavkar Saheb, Assistant Director Shri Chandrakant Dhekne Saheb Regional Office of Vocational Education and Training, Pune, District Vocational Education and Training Officer Sachin Dhumal Saheb and Headmaster Government Technical School Kendra Shalmali Pawar Madam and son Adhiraj Dole, mother Kusum Dole, I am very grateful to my father Madhukar Dole and wife Ashwini Dole for their special guidance and cooperation from time to time.

Also, in a very short period of time, the book was reviewed by Shri Rajendra Ghume Saheb, Joint Director, Vocational Education and Training Regional Office, Pune, for his invaluable time in publishing the book. I am sincerely grateful for their feedback.

I am grateful to the Instructor of ITI Satara for there continuous support from the very beginning of writing the book.

From this book, I consider myself blessed to have shared my thoughts on e-learning with you. I will not claim that this book is perfect, because considering the perfection, this book is an attempt and is in its infancy. They will be valuable for improvement if they are tested and suggested.

Manoj Dole
Dated 9/1/2019

Acknowledgements

The industrial training and theoretical examination system of our industrial training institutes and these changes have been accepted by the craft instructors and the trainees. Theoretical examinations conducted in your industrial training institutes are also conducted online. Since these examinations are of multiple choice MCQ method, the trainees will need to get more practice of such questions.

With all these considerations in mind, Mr. Manoj Madhukar, Director, Dole Crafts, Katari Industrial Training Institute, Satara, has done a thorough study and with his diligent work and added his keen intellect, according to the new annual system and NSQF-5 syllabus, e-book of Katari and other machine trades. -Book) and they have created mobile apps and blogs on theoretical topics to make training easier and have made all these educational materials available for download on the world famous websites Google Play Store, Amazon and Apple Book Store. Training has been made easier by creating a print version and using advanced techniques like QR Code.

All these educational materials will definitely be a guide for all the trainees for in-depth study and for the craft instructors and other concerned who are imparting vocational training.

CHAPTER ONE

Draughtsman Civil First Year QR Code Images

Download App
Online Test Exam
ITI Books
AutoCAD CAM
JOB & Apprentice
Online Theory
Computer Course
Trading Course
CNC Course
MSCIT Course
Shopping Business
Internet Business
Web Designing
Online Services
Top Sportsmans
Indian Army
Freedom Fighters
Top Scientists
Social Reformers
Motivational Speaker
Top Richest People
Join WhatsApp Group
Join Facebook Group
Like Facebook Page
PAN / Adhar / Licence
Passport

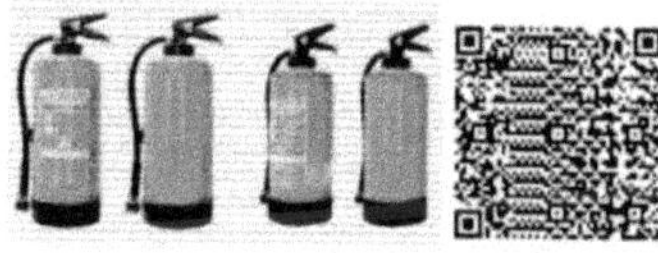

Fire extinguisher

French curve in drawing

Set square in drawing

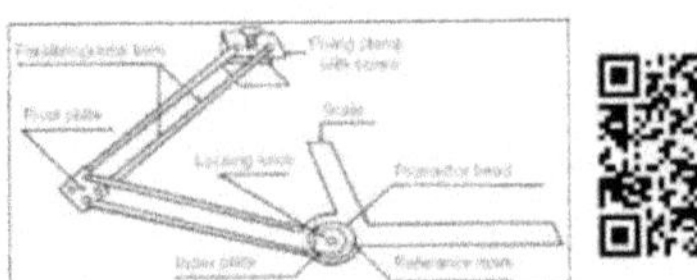

Mini drafter in drawing

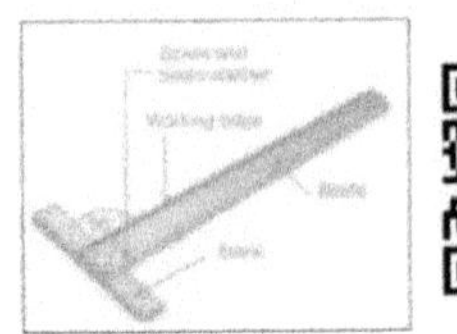

T - square in drawing

Orthographic projection in drawing

Third angle projection drawing

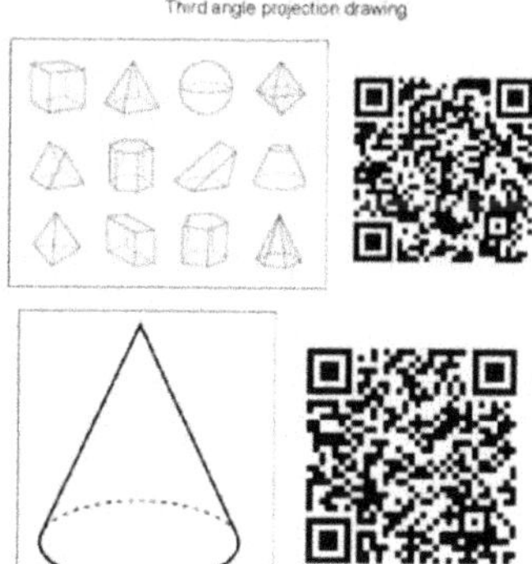

Cone in engineering drawing

Sphere in drawing

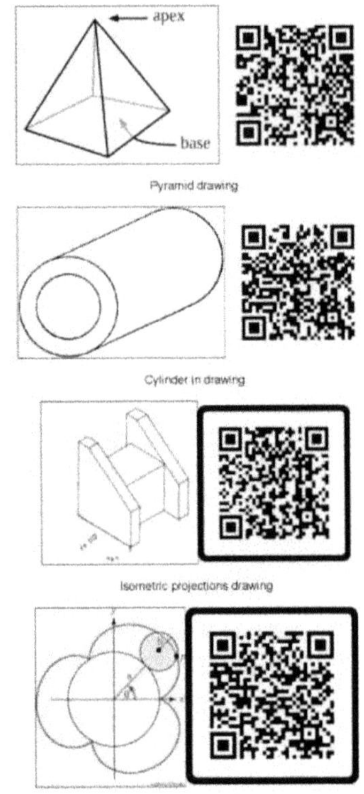

Pyramid drawing

Cylinder in drawing

Isometric projections drawing

Curves engineering drawing

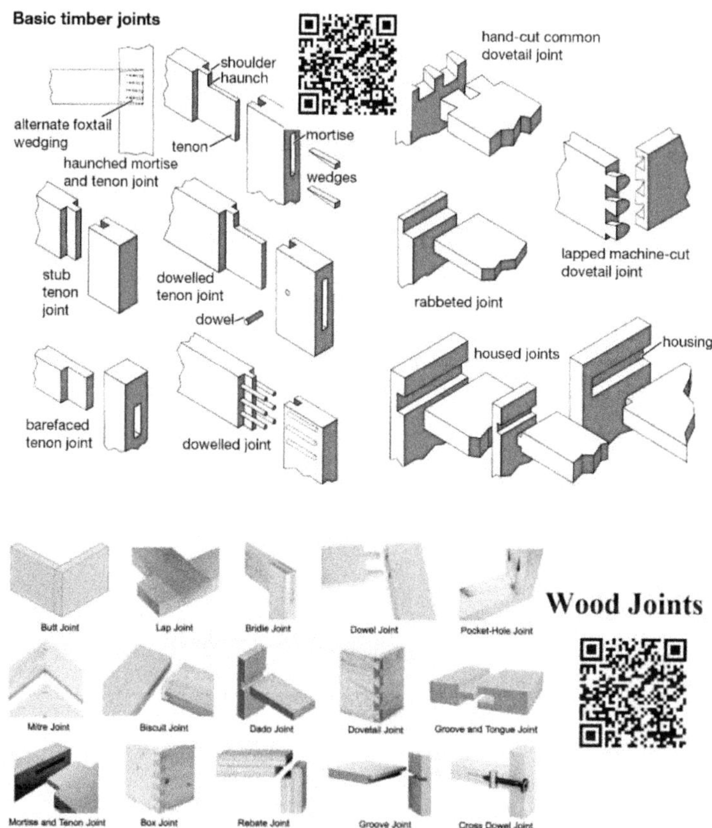
Basic timber joints
shoulder
haunch
alternate foxtail wedging
tenon
haunched mortise and tenon joint
mortise
wedges
hand-cut common dovetail joint
stub tenon joint
dowelled tenon joint
dowel
rabbeted joint
lapped machine-cut dovetail joint
housed joints
housing
barefaced tenon joint
dowelled joint
Wood Joints
Butt Joint
Lap Joint
Bridle Joint
Dowel Joint
Pocket-Hole Joint
Mitre Joint
Biscuit Joint
Dado Joint
Dovetail Joint
Groove and Tongue Joint
Mortise and Tenon Joint
Box Joint
Rebate Joint
Groove Joint
Cross Dowel Joint

CHAPTER TWO

Draughtsman Civil First Year MCQ

01] In case of bleeding, take treatment Of

D] cold 3" and rest

A] spray cold water

B] Bandage immediately -----.

B] Enquire about the accident thought treatment

02] in case of an accident, the victim should im

A] Asked to take rest

C] Attended immediately

D] leave him

03] First aid is given to an injured or ill person primarily....

A] Save life

B] Prevent further deterioration of the muff's

C] Give best possible comfort

D] All of these

04] Colour code for Bins for waste paper segregation is -----

A] blue Colour

B] Yellow Colour

C] Red Colour

D] Green Colour

05] In Japanese Seiko stands for -------------

A] Shine

B] Sort

C] Standardize

D] Sustain

06] Benefit of SS system is ------

A] Increase in productivity

B] Increase in quality

C] Reduction in wastage of time

D] All of these

07] Safety is -----------

A] nobody's business

B] every bodise business

C] Some bodies business

D] The organization business

08] For basic categories of safety signs are available The meaning of"prohibition" sign ----

A] shows it must not be done

B] Shows what must be done

C] Warns the hazard or danger

D] Gives information of safety provision

09] Which one is a workshop safety?

A] Keep shop floor clean and free from grease, oil or other slippery materials

B] Stop the machine before changing the speed

C] Don't use cracked or chipped tools

D] Don't try to stop a running machine with hand

10] In Personal Protect Equipment (PPE] HELMET is used to

A] protect head

B] Protect eyes

C] Protect hands

D] Protect ears

11] Which of the following belongs to general safety?

A Have a worker in good attitude

B] The work clean and clear

C] Concentrate on your work

D] Keep the floor and gangways clean and clear

13] Which of the following is done for machine safety?

A] Check the oil level before starting the machine

B] Do things in a methodical way

C] Keep the floor and gangways clean and clear

D] Don't use dies and scarves

14] In Personal Protect Equipment (PPE] , 'sleeves' is used to protect ----------

A] Face

B] Eyes
C] Ears
D] Hands
15] ABC stands for --------------
A] Automatic Breathing Control
B] Automatic Blood Control
C] Airway Breathing Circulation
D] Automatic Blood Circulation
16] To put off"Class B" fire, the types of fire extinguisher used is ....
A] dry power
B] Carbon dioxide
C] Jet of water
D] Foam type
17] Which type of fire extinguisher is used to put off general fire?
A] Water type Extinguisher
B] Foam type Extinguisher
C] Dry chemical powder Extinguisher
D] Carbon dioxide (C02] Extinguisher

Fire extinguisher

18]The 'T' square is used for drawing lines ......
a] inclined
b] curved
c] vertical
d] horizontal
19] For drawing large size circle is drawn by.....
a] straight bar
b] lengthening bar
c] big bar
d] small bar
20] To draw or measure angle is used by.....

a]set square

b] protractor

c] 'T' square

d] none of these

21] The grade of pencil is used to sketching lettering ....

a] conical point

b] chisel point

c] soft

d] low

22] For drawing thin lines of uniform thickness the pencil should be sharpened in the form of ....

a] chisel edge

b]conical

c] pointed

d] none of these

23] What is used for drawing curves which can not drawn by compass

a] small compass

b] French curve

c] protractor

d] none of these

French curve in drawing

24]Unnecessary lines is removed by .....

a] Duster

b] sand paper block

c] eraser

d] none of these

25] Circle and arcs are drawn by means of .....l.

a] compass

b] divider

c] lengthening bar

d]none of these

26] Inking pen is used in drawing ......

a] horizontal line

b] non circular arcs

c] vertical lines

d] all of these

27] The card board scale are available in set of .....

a] 7

b] 8

c] 6

d] 9

28] The convenient length size of 30 -60°-90° set square for used in school and colleges are......

a] 250

b] 200

c] 300

d] none of these

Set square in drawing

29] Drawing board is shape of ....

a] square

b] rectangular

c] triangular

d] none of these

30] The ‘T’ square , set square ,scale protractor are complain use in.......

a] protractor

b] mini drafter

c] set square

d] none of these

Mini drafter in drawing

31]Set square , T square edges are bevelled for the purpose of....

a] curve line

b] inking lines

b] taking measurements

d] none of these

T - square in drawing

32]Geometrical construction which are mostly based on plane geometry and which are very.......

a] Accuracy

b] Quality

c] Essential

d] Superior quality

33] How much method of drawing the regular polygons.......

a] Inscribe circle method and arc method

b] General method for drawing any polygon

c] Alternative method

d] All of these

34] The line AB can be divided into .... equal parts.

a] 7

b] 10

c] 15

d] All of them

35] Which method of constructing triangl in circle......

a] Inscribing

b] Describing

c] Both a and b

d] None of these

36] When two sides of the hexagon are required to be horizontal the starting point for stepping equal division should be on an end of the.....

a] Horizontal diameter

b] Vertical diameter

c] Inclined diameter

d] None of these

37] If two sides of hexagon are required to be vertical the starting point should be on an end of the....

a] Inclined diameter

b] Horizontal diameter

c] Vertical diameter

d] None of these

38] The section obtained by the inter section of the right circular cone by a plane in different position relative to the axis of the cone are called.......

a] Conics

b] Circles

c] Triangles

d] Half circle

58] The lines from the object to the plane are called.......

a] Projection

b] Projector

c] Reference plane

d] None of these

59] The orthographic projection an object is represented by View on the mutual perpendicular projection lines

a] Two or three

b] Three or two

c] Three or four

d] None of these

60] When the projectors are parallel to each other & also perpendicular to the plane, the projection is called......

a] Isometric projection

b] Oblique projection

c] Orthographic projection

d] Perspective projection

Orthographic projection in drawing

61] The two planes employed for the purpose of Orthographic projections are......

a] Auxillary plane

d] Horizontal plane

c] Reference plane

d] None of these

62] The line in which they intersect is termed the reference line & is denoted by the letters.......

a] AB

b] YZ

c] XY

d] None of these

63] The projection on the VP is called........

a] Side view

b] Front view

c] Top view

d] All of these

64] ....Method, when the views are drawn in their relative positions, the plane comes below the elevation. The view of the object as observed from the left-side the right of elevation.

a] Plane of projection

b] First angle projection

c] Third angle projection

d] None of these

65] Third angle projection method, the object is assumed to be situated in the........ quadrant.

a] First quadrant

b] Second quadrant

c] Third quadrant

d] Fourth quadrant

66] .... Method of projection is used in U.S.A & also in other countries.

a] plane of projection

b] Orthographic projection

c] First-angle projection

d] Third angle projection

Third angle projection drawing

67] When an object is situated on the ground, in first angle projection method, the bottom of its ..... will co-inside with XY

a] Top view

b] Front view

c] side view

d] All of these

68] The important element of this projection system

a] An object

b] Plane of projection

c] An observer

d] All of these

69] When line AB is parallel to HP hence ....

a] It' front view to AB

b] It''s side view equal to AB

c] It's top view equal to AB

d] None of these

70] When a line is parallel to a plane; it's projection on plane is equal to it's ;

a] True length

b] True shape

c] True size

d] None of these

71] The point is parallel in which the line or line produced meet the point is plane is called it's ....

a] Line

b] ratio

c] Trace

d] none of these

72] .... is the shortest distance between two points.

a] a line

b] a point

c] a straight line

d] none of these

73] When the line intersect horizontal plane that's called.....

a] horizontal trace

b] vertical trace

c] trace of line

d] none of these

74]Planes may be divided into two main types ......

a] Perpendicular planes, auxillary planes

b] Perpendicular plane, oblique planes

c] Auxillary planes , perpendicular planes

d] none of these

75] Planes which are inclined to the reference plane are called......

a] Auxillary plane

b] obliqeu plane

c] Perpendicular planes

d] picture plane

76] When a plane is perpendicular to a reference plane it's projection on that plane is a..........

a] horizontal line

b] parallel line

c] straight line

d] none of these

77] When a plane is parallel to a reference plane , it's projection on that plane shows........

a] It's true shape &size

b] It's true length & size

c] It's true height & size

d] none of these

78] Plane perpendicular to VP & HP that plane is called as ....

a] Auxillary Plane

b] Oblique Plane

c] Perpendicular Plane

d] None of these

79] Perpendicular plane can be divides into the following types.........

a] Perpendicular to both the reference planes.

b] Perpendicular to one plane & parallel to other

c] Perpendicular to one plane & inclined to other

d] All of these

80] The planes have only two dimensions, viz........

a] Length & breadth

b] Length & height

c] Length & thickness

d] All of these

81] The imaginary line of prism joining the centrs of the bases called.........

a] Faces

b] Axis

c] Apex

d] Base

82] A right & regular prism has it's axis....... to the bases

a] Parallel

b] Perpendicular

c] Inclined

d] None of these

83] When a pyramid or a cone is cut by a plane parallel to it's base thus removing the top portion, the remaining portion is called it's.........

a] Sphere

b] Cone

c] Cylinder

d] Frustum

Cone in engineering drawing

84] Oblique cylinder & cones have their axes........ to their base

a] Inclined

b] Parallel

c] Perpendicular

d] All of these

85] Projection of two equal sphere s resting on the ground & in contact with each other, with the line joining there centre parallel to the..........

a] A VP

b] VP

c] HP

d] All of these

Sphere in drawing

86] Projections of section on the other plane to which it is inclined is called.......

a] Section planes

b] Apparent section

c] True shape of sphere

d] None of these

87] When the section plane is parallel to the HP or the ground, the true shape of the section will be seen in.........

a] Front view

b] Side view

c] Top view

d] All of these

88] Surface of solid are laid out on a plane the figure obtained is called its........

a] Interpenetration

b] Development

c] Intersection

d] None of these

89] Development of surfaces is essential in.........

a] Foundry shop

b] Sheet metal work

c] Fitting shop

d] None of these

90] Which method of development used in transition pieces?

a] Parallel diameter

b] Radial line method

c] Triangulation method

d] Approximate method

91] Which method of development used in pyramids and cones.........

a] Radial line method

b] Parallel line method

c] Approximate method

d] Triangulation method

Pyramid drawing

92] Parallel line method is used in..........

a] Prism

b] Cylinder

c] Cubes

d] All of these

93] Which method of development used in surface as sphere, paraboloid, ellipsoid, hyperboloid, and helicoids

a] Radial line method

b] Triangulation method

c] Approximate method

d] Parallel line method

94] Zone method and lune method is used in development of........

a] Prisms

b] Cones

c] Sphere

d] Pyramids

95] Calculation the subtended angle Θ by the formula Θ =360^0 $_\times$ radius of the base circle

a] Length of axis

b] Slant height

c] Radius of axis

d] None of these

96] In engineering practice, objects constructed may have constituent part, the surfaces of which intersect one another in lines called........ of intersection.

a] Lines

b] Cones

c] Cylinder
d] Prisms

97] The line of interaction may be depending upon the nature of.......
a] Intersection surface
b] Intersecting solids
c] Intersection cones
d] None of these

98] The two plane surface intersect in a........ line
a] Curve
b] Straight
c] Plane
d] All of these

99] The line of intersection between two curved surface or between......... Surface and a curved surface is a curve.
a] A curved
b] A plane
c] A solids
d] None of these

100] When a solids completely penetration another solids there will be two lines of intersection. These lines are sometimes called the line or........
a] Line of interpenetration
b] Curve of interpenetration
c] Solids of interpenetration
d] All of these

101] Use of penetration curve is.......
a] Sheet metal work
b] Fitting shop
c] Fabricating work
d] Foundry shop

102] Methods of determining the line of intersection between surface of two interpenetration.........
a] Approximate method & radial line method
b] Line method and cutting plane method
c] Triangulation method and parallel line method
d] None of these

103] Example of interpenetration is..........
a] Two prism intersection
b] Cylinder and prism intersection

c] Cone and cylinders intersection

d] All of these

104] Two cylinder intersection is example of.........

a] Intersection

b] Interpenetration

c] Cone intersection

d] None of these

Cylinder in drawing

105] .... Method is explained in detail while solving illustrative problems

a] Line method

b] Radial line method

c] Cutting plane method

d] Parallel line method

106] What is a type of isometric projection?

a] Pictorial projection

b] Orthographic projection

c] Perspective projection

d] Oblique Projection

Isometric projections drawing

107] Isometric views have been drawn........

a] Full scale

b] Half scale

c] True length

d] True scale

108] The line parallel to isometric axis are called........

a] Isometric axis

b] Isometric line

c] Isometric planes

d] Isometric views

109] The isometric projection is reduce in the ratio.........

a] 3]

b] 1] 2

c] 2] 2

d] 2] 3

110] The isometric projection of circle drawn with........

a] Isometric Plane

b] Isometric graph

c] Isometric Drawing

d] Isometric Scale

111] The major axis of the ellipse is long than...............

a] Radius of the circle

b] True diameter

c] Diameter of the circle

d] None of these

112] Makes practice for drawing of isometric view using........

a] Isometric planes

b] Isometric lines

c] Isometric graph

d] Isometric view

3] What is the term of the outermost layer of earth

A] Lithosphere

B] Atmosphere

C] Hydrosphere

D] Thermosphere

4] Which is the most accepted method of avoiding accident

A] Wearing safety equipment

B] Doing things in one s own way

C] Performing with highly skilled working practice _

D] Observing safety precautions related to job, machine and working place ,

5] What is class D fire class

A] Oil and fats

B] Flammable liquids

C] Combustible metals

D] Energized electrical equipment

6] What is ABC of first aid

A] Aid, break, control , ,

B] Avoid, bleeding, control

C] Airway, breathing, circulation

D] Accident, bleeding, circulation

7] What is the percentage of oxygen in atmospheric gases

A] 78.03 %

B] 20.99 %

C] 15.88%

D] 12.41 %

8] How occupational disease caused in industrial environment

A] Negligence

B] Lack of knowledge

C] Impropcr handling of machincs

D] Persons exposed to substance or process

9] What is the designation of 420 x 594 mm size paper as per BIS

A] A1

B] A2

C] A3

D] A4

10] What is the part of a circle bounded by two radii on its arc

A] Circle

B] Sector

C] Segment

D] Semi-circle -

12] What is the name of the dimensioning arrangement

A] Chain dimensioning
B] Parallel dimensioning
C] Aligned dimensioning
D] Unidirectional dimensioning
13] What is the name of scale

A] Plain scale
B] Vernier scale
C] Diagonal scale
D] Comparative scale
14] What is the name of part labeled as x

A] Plug
B] Fuse head
C] Base charge
D] Priming charge
15] What is the name of dressing of stone

A] Dragged finish
B] Furrowed finish
C] Reticulated finish
D] Hammer dressed finish
16] Name the arrow pointed in spacing of drawing sheet.

A] Trimming edge
B] Border
C] Orientation mark
D] Frame
17] What the arrow hcad dcnotcs

A] Battens
B] Strips
C] Ebony edge
D] Holder
18] What is the part marked as x X

A] Screw
B] Head
C] Blade
D] Linkage
19] What is the angle between the stock / head and blade in T- square
A] 30°
B] 45°
C] 60°
D] 90°
20] What is A4 designation for untrimmed size of drawing sheet
A] 450 x 625 mm
B] 330 x 450 mm
C] 240 x 330 mm
D] 165 x 240 mm
21] What is the material for given symbol

A] Stone
B] Partition block
C] Cone
D] Brick
22] Which is the object for given symbol

A] Rolling shutter internal
B] Sliding door internal
C] Sliding door external
D] Rolling shutter external

23] Which BIS code no is recommended for folding of drawing sheets

A] IS 11664 - 1989

B] IS 11664 - 1987

C] IS 11664 - 1986

D] IS 11664 – 1981

24] How many vertical folds come under 'A0' size trimmed drawing sheet

A] 5

B] 6

C] 7

D] 8

24a] What is the untrimmed size of A5 designation drawing sheet

A] 450 x 625

B] 330 x 450

C] 240 x 330

D] 165 x 240

25] What is the size / height in mm for material list and dimensioning in drawings

A] 9 to 10

B] 7 to 8

C] 5 to 6

D] 3 to 4

26] What is the discription of E1 hidden outlines E1

A] Dashed thin

B] Chain thin

C] Dashed thick

D] Chain thick

27] How the dimensions can be read in aligned system of dimension technique

A] Left hand edge of drawing sheet

B] Right hand edge of drawing sheet

C] Top to bottom

D] Bottom to top

28] What is the description of 'G1' in centre line

A] Chain thin

B] Dashed thin

C] Dashed thick

D] Continuous thick

28-1] How the unidirectional system dimensions are placed in engineering drawing to read

A] From the top of the drawing

B] From left side to right

C] From the bottom of drawing

D] From right side to left

29] What is the size / Height in mm for sub - titles of drawing

A] 3 - 5

B] 6 - 8

C] 9 - 10

D] 11 - 12

30] What is the scale used generally in MAPS

A] 1]108

B] 1]107

C] 1]106

D] 1]105

31] What is the R.F, if an actual length of distance 5 m represented by 25 mm length

A] 1]2000

B] 1]200

C] 1]20

D] 1]2

32] What is the name of given scale

A] Plain

B] Comparative

C] Vernier

D] Diagonal

33] Which scale is used to construct angles in absence of a protractor

A] Diagonal scale

B] Comparative scale

C] Chord scale

D] Plain scale

34] What is the given scale

A] Plain scale

B] Comparative scale

C] Diagonal scale

D] Vernier scale

35] What is the classification of igneous rock

A] Geological

B] Physical

C] Chemical

D] Practical

36] Which lime is used for construction of masonry

A] Class D

B] Class C

C] Class B

D] Class A

37] How many grades the ordinary port land cement is available as per IS specification

A] 2 grades

B] 3 grades

C] 4 grades

D] 5 grades

38] What is the percentage of cement water proofer in powder form for all water refining structure

A] 13 to 15%

B] 11 to 12%

C] 06 to 10%

D] 02 to 05%

39] What is the projection if the receding lines are drawn to ½ scale

A] Cavalier projection

B] Cabinet projection

C] Clirographic projection

D] Axonometric projection

40] What is the part marked as x

A] Blocking course
B] Cornile
C] Cortel
D] Lintel
41] What is the part marked as x X

A] Corbel
B] Blocking course
C] String course
D] Frieze course
42] What is the part marked as x

A] Corbel course
B] Cornice course
C] Blocking course
D] String course
43] Which rock has a main content of silica

A] Argillaceous rock
B] Siliceous rock
C] Calcareous rock
D] Foliated rock
44] What is the classification of marble
A] Metamorphic rock
B] Foliated rock
C] Sedimentary rock
D] Igneous rock
45] What is the name of stone dressing finish

A] Boasted finish
B] Dragged finish
C] Dragged finish
D] Polished finish
46] What is the colour code for brick materials
A] Vermilion
B] Cobalt blue
C] Payers grey
D] Harbors green
47] What is the name of the symbol

A] Cutting
B] Embankment
C] Culvert
D] Bridge
48] What is the name of the scale that is denoted by 5] 1
A] Full scale
B] Plain scale
C] Reduced scale
D] Enlarged scale

49] What is the name of the test that to determine the durability or weathering quality

A] Impact test

B] Smith's test

C] Crushing test

D] Crystallization test

49a] Which quadrilateral has all the sides are equal and angles are not at right angles

A] Rhombus

B] Trapezoid

C] Rectangle

D] Rhomboid

50] What is designation of drawing sheet used in 700 x 500 x 15 mm size drawing board

A] A0

B] A1

C] A2

D] A3

51] What is the maximum degree can be measured in circular protractor

A] 360°

B] 270°

C] 180°

D] 390°

52] What is the process in manufacturing of bricks if the clay is made lose and any ingredient to be added to it ,

A] Weathering

B] Cleaning

C] Tempering

D] Blending

53] Which rock has main content of calcium carbonate

A] Argillaceous rocks

B] Siliceous rocks

C] Foliated rocks

D] Calcareous rocks

54] Where the rear view is placed in first angle projection

A] Right side of right side view

B] Bottom of elevation

C] Left side of right side view

D] Top of elevation

55] Where the plan is placed in third angle projection

A] Below elevation

B] Above elevation

C] Left of elevation

D] Right of elevation

56] What is the property of material to absorb water vapour from air

A] Hydroscopicity

B] Water absorption

C] Permeability

D] Durability

57] What is known as the capacity of material to permit water to pass through it under pressure

A] Durability

B] Permeability

C] Porosity

D] Ductility

58] Which test is conducted on stone to study minor constituents grain size

A] Freezing

B] Smiths

C] Microscopic test

D] Hardness

59] Name the process of removing about 20 cm depth of soil to a certain area for manufacturing of brick

A] Unsoiling

B] Tempering

C] Blending

D] Cleaning

60] What is marked as x in brickwork

A] Cornice brick

B] Bullnose brick

C] Cant brick

D] Round ended brick

61] Which test is conducted to know the classification of lime

A] Ball test
B] Visual test
C] Impurity test
D] Workability test
62] Which is the test done using vicat apparatus
A] Fineness test
B] Compressive strength test
C] Soundness test
D] Tensile strength test
63] What is the percentage gypsum added in manufacture of cement
A] 7 - 10%
B] 5 -7 %
C] 3 to 4 %
D] 1 - 2 %
64] Which cement is more suitable for the construction of chemical plant and furnace
A] Expanding cement
B] High alumina cement
C] Extra rapid hardening cement
D] Hydrophobic cement
65] What is the proportion of cement water proofers for water tanks in paste form
A] 1 to 10
B] 11 to 15
C] 16 to 20
D] 21 to 25
66] Which cement is more suitable for construction of abutment and piers
A] High alumina cement
B] Rapid hardening cement
C] Modified port land cement

D] Sulphate resisting cement

67] What is the name of the part labelled as x

A] Pith

B] Bast

C] Sap wood

D] Heart wood

68] What is the name of form labelled as x in bricks masonry

A] Header

B] Quoin closer

C] Queen closer

D] Quoin stretcher

69] Which type of paint is applied for iron work under water

A] Asbestos paint

B] Cellulose paint

C] Aluminium paint D] Bituminous paint

70] What is the name of stone joint

A] Lap joint

B] Butt joint

C] Tabled joint

D] Tongue and groove joint

71] What is the name of brick

A] King closer
B] Bevelled bat
C] Queen closer
D] Mitered closer
72] What is the name of the wall

A] Stone facing with backing
B] Stone facing with rubble backing
C] Brick facing with concrete backing
D] Facing of brick works and backing of ashlar masonry
73] What is the name of tool used for setting `angle in brick masonry `
A] Bevel
B] Plumb rule
C] Masons square
D] 1 meter 'U' folded rule 1 'U '
73a] Which rigid board is known as pressed board
A] Plywood board
B] Compreg board
C] Fibre board
D] Laminated board
74] Which surfaces are recommended with cement paint, emulsion paint, oilpaint and silverate paint
A] Iron surface
B] Plastered surface
C] Wood surface
D] Metal surface

75] What is the term used for covering or killings of all knots in wood surface by red lead A] Finishing B] Knotting C] Stopping D] Cleaning

76] Which metal consists of copper and tin

A] Bronze

B] Brass

C] Dow metal

D] Nickel silver

77] What is the part marked as x X

A] Coping

B] Parapet

C] Throating

D] D.P.C

78] What is the name of brick

A] Cellular clay brick

B] Hollow clay brick

C] Hollow concrete brick

D] Perforated brick

79] Which is the market form of timber with parallel sides having thickness less than 50 mm and its width exceed 50 mm

A] Plank

B] Pole

C] Deal

D] Bulk

80] What is the process of removing moisture present in freshly felled timber

A] Hardening

B] Stiffing

C] Sapping

D] Seasoning

81] What is the artificial seasoning while timber immersed in a solution of suitable salt

A] Chemical seasoning

B] Electrical seasoning

C] Water seasoning

D] Kiln seasoning

82] What is the defect due to seasoning in timber

A] Cup

B] Bow

C] Split

D] Warp

83] What is the use of thin sheets of wood varies from 0.4 mm to 6 mm thickness

A] Plywood

B] Fibre board

C] Laminated board

D] Veneers

84] Which is the smaller timber block up to 25mm width used for construction of bus bodies and marines

A] Laminated board

B] Fibre board

C] Plywood

D] Block board

85] What is the process of surface smoothened by rubbing with sand paper or pumic stone for varnishing

A] Application of surface
B] Preparation of surface
C] Cleaning of surface
D] Finishing of surface
86] What is the term used for the pores on the surface are filled up with boiled linseed oil
A] Grining
B] Stopping
C] Knotting
D] Sagging
87] Which metal has content of aluminium alloy 94% copper 4%
A] Brass
B] Bronze
C] Dow bell
D] Duralumin
88] What for the corrugated sheet form of steel in mostly used
A] Structural work
B] Roof covering
C] Grillwork
D] Reinforce cement concrete
89] What is the part marked as x in masonry

A] Header
B] Quoin
C] Bed joint
D] Stretcher
90] What is the part marked as x

A] Queen closer
B] Stretcher
C] Header

D] Quoin

91] What is marked as x in masonry x

A] Stretcher

B] Bed joint

C] Quoin closer

D] Quoin

92] What is the stone joint used in stone masonry

A] Plugged joint

B] Rusticated joint

C] Tabled joint

D] Butt joint

93] What is the stone joint used in stone masonry

A] Saddled joint

B] Butt joint

C] Tabled joint

D] Butt joint

94] Which stone joint is used in arch work

A] Butt joint

B] Table joint

C] Rebated joint

D] Joggled joint

95] Which masonry has provision for clamps or dowels between facing and backing of wall

A] Stone masonry

B] Brick masonry

C] Brick masonry in mud mortar

D] Composite masonry

96] What is the name of masonry

A] Dry rubble masonry

B] Random rubble masonry

C] Coursed rubble masonry

D] Coursed rubble masonry

99] What is the stone masonry

A] Ashlar rock

B] Ashlar rough tooled

C] Ashlar fine

D] Ashlar chamfered

100] What is the joint used in stone masonry

A] Rebated joint

B] Butt joint

C] Tabled joint

D] Tongued and grooved

101] Which stone joint is used for coping

A] Tabled joint

B] Plugged joint

C] Joggled joint

D] Cramped joint

102] Which masonry has regular stones of square or rectangular shape with accurate bed joints

A] Coursed R.B .. B] Uncoursed Rubble masonry

C] Ashlar fine masonry

D] Flint rubble masonry

103] What is the name of bond used in masonry

A] English cross wall bond

B] Dutch bond

C] Facing bond

D] Racking bond

104] What is the part marked as x in brick course

A] Rear Wythe Wythe

B] Stretcher course

C] Front Wythe

D] Header course

105] What is the bond used in masonry

A] Diagonal bond

B] Garden wall (English) bond

C] Monk bond

D] Single Flemish bond

106] What is the form of connection in brick work if the enclosed angle on the side of the wall should be between 90° to 180°

A] Squint quoin

B] Acute squint quoin

C] Right led

D] Obtuse squint quoin

107] Which bond consists of alternate courses of headers and stretchers

A] Monk bond

B] Racking bond

C] Dutch bond D] Facing bond

108] What is the name of bond

A] Rat trap bond

B] Brick on edge bond

C] Flemish (Single) bond

D] Flemish (Double) bond

109] What is the name of the defect in timber

A] Knot

B] Cup shakes

C] Star shakes

D] Radial shakes

110] What is the dead load

A] Roof

B] Snow

C] Wind pressure

D] Men and animals

111] What is the name of tool

A] Shell auger

B] Screw auger

C] Post-hole auger

D] Wash boring auger

112] What is the name of foundation

A] Raft footing

B] Strap footing

C] Rectangular footing

D] Trapezoidal footing

113] What is the name of the foundation that is due to heavy inflow seepage and not possible to excavate the trenches and keep them dry

A] Pile foundation

B] Raft foundation

C] Spread foundation

D] Shallow foundation

114] What is the name of the piles that are driven at an inclination to resist large horizontal or inclined forces

A] Batter piles

B] Sheet piles

C] Anchor piles

D] Fender piles

115] What is the machine foundation bolt

A] Eye bolt
B] Rag bolt
C] Lewis bolt
D] Cotter bolt
116] What is the footing for heavy loaded column that require greater spread
A] Wall footing
B] Sloped footing
C] Spread footing
D] Stepped footing
117] Which type of foundation is recommended for black cotton soil
A] Raft foundation
B] Strap foundation
C] Spread footing foundation
D] Stepped footing foundation
119] What is ro in the formula for determining UBC of soil = ro
A] Factor of safety
B] Density of soil at depth
C] Ultimate load on unit area
D] Resistance of soil / unit area
121] What is the minimum distance between building and a tree
A] 8 m
B] 6 m
C] 5 m
D] 4 m
122] What is the weight range of sand (dry) in Kg/m3

A] 1000 to 1500
B] 1540 to 1600
C] 1600 to 1700
D] 1700 to 1800
123] What is the name of foundation

A] Wall footing
B] Strap footing
C] Rectangular footing
D] Single footing
124] What is known as the spread footing for a single column
A] Stepped footing
B] Single footing
C] Slopped footing
D] Pad footing
125] What is a spread footing that supports two columns
A] Strap footing foundation
B] Rectangular Combined footing foundation
C] Wall footing foundation
D] Single footing foundation
126] What is the name of pile

A] Pre cast concrete pile
B] Friction pile
C] Batter pile
D] End bearing pile

127] What is known as a structure that is sunk through water / ground to exclude water during the process of excavation of foundation

A] Cofferdam

B] Under reamed pile foundation

C] Caisson

D] Strip / Pad foundation

128] Which method of soil exploration is suitable for a depth of 3m

A] Open excavation

B] Probing

C] Wash boring

D] Auger boring

129] Which is suitable depth open excavation method of site exploration is suitable A] 1.5 m

B] 2.5 m

C] 3.0 m

D] 3.5 m

130] Which method of Soil exploration is essential to test soil for the construction of Dam/Engineering structures

A] Sub surface sounding method

B] Geophysical method

C] Deep boring method

D] Wash boring method

131] Which method of soil exploration is suitable to find the depth of bed rock or stratum A] Sub surface sounding method

B] Geophysical method

C] Wash boring method

D] Auger boring method

132] Which method of site exploration is suitable for a depth of 6 to 8 m range A] Test pit

B] Probing

C] Auger boring

D] Wash boring

133] Which soil observation method belongs to Seismic refraction method

A] Sub surface sounding method

B] Deep boring method

C] Wash boring method

D] Geophysical method

134] Which soil observation method belongs to Electrical resistivity

A] Deep boring B] Wash boring

C] Geophysical

D] Sub surface sounding

135] What is the maximum safe bearing capacity of hard rock without defect (say in T/m2) A] 250

B] 270

C] 300

D] 330

136] Which method of shut piles are driven in the ground and therefore the bearing B.C of soil is increased

A] Drainage of soil method

B] Continuing soil method C] Compacting soil method

D] Grouting soil method

137] Which method of improving B.C of soil is useful for bearing stratum is met at greater depth

A] Grouting method

B] Compacting soil method

C] Increasing the (Depth) of foundation method

D] Drainage of soil method

138] Which method of Soil exploration is suitable for testing cohesion less soil

A] Auger boring method

B] Sub surface sounding method

C] Deep boring method

D] Wash boring method

139] Which method determining bearing capacity of soil by Rankine s formula

A] Method of dropping a weight

B] Method of loading

C] Arithmetical method

D] Analytical method

140] What is the general value of factor of safety range to find B C of soil

A] 0.25 - 0.40

B] 0.40 - 0.80

C] 0.80 - 1.00

D] 2 - 3

141] What is the super imposed material load in Kg/m2 for office and churches A] 400

B] 350

C] 300

D] 250

142] What is the weight range of brick in Kg/m3 Kg/m3

A] 1400 - 1440

B] 1440 - 1550 C] 1600 - 1920

D] 2000 – 2100

143] What is the recommended super imposed load material in Kg/m2 for public building and dance hall

A] 500

B] 450

C] 400

D] 350

144] What is the weight range of dry earth in Kg/m3 Kg/m3

A] 1000 - 1200

B] 1200 - 1300

C] 1300 - 1400

D] 1410 – 1840

145] What is the weight of plain cement concrete in Kg/m3 Kg/m3

A] 2300

B] 2500

C] 2700

D] 2800

146] What is the recommended super imposed material load in Kg/m2 for residential and hospital buildings

A] 400 Kg/m2

B] 250 Kg/m2

C] 300 Kg/m2

D] 350 Kg/m2

147] What is the recommended super imposed load in Kg/m2 for work house and book stalls

A] 800

B] 900

C] 1000

D] 1200

148] What is the weight of steel in Kg/m3

A] 7250
B] 7500
C] 7850
D] 8000

149] What is the recommended super imposed load in Kg/m2 for heavy Workshop and factories

A] 500
B] 550
C] 650
D] 750

150] What is the name of foundation, if the foundation s depth is less than (or) equal to its width

A] Deep foundation
B] Will foundation
C] Pier foundation
D] Shallow foundation

151] What is the name of foundation

A] Single footing
B] Stepped footing
C] Slopped footing
D] Wall footing without step

152] What is the centre to centre distance range between the beams in timber grillage foundation

A] 35 to 40 cm
B] 40 to 45 cm

C] 45 to 50 cm

D] 50 to 60 cm

153] Which type of foundation footings rectangular / trepezoidal in plan

A] Strap footing foundation

B] Slopped footing foundation

C] Combined footing foundation

D] Wall footing foundation

154] Which type of foundation used in olden days for the construction of bridges and tanks

A] Combined footing foundation

B] Continuous foundation

C] Spread footing foundation

D] Inverted arch foundation

155] Which foundation is suitable, if the Safe bearing capacity of soil is very low and it is required to distribute heavy concentrated load over a large area

A] Raft foundation

B] Inverted arch foundation

C] Combined footing

D] Grillage foundation

156] What is the name of foundation given in Plan'

A] Cantilever foundation

B] Continuous footing foundation

C] Combined footing foundation

D] Spread footing foundation

156a] Which foundation has 80 cm pipe is embedded at plinth level connecting to foundation bottom (above 5 cm) with an internal of 1.5 m approximately

A] Combined footing foundation

B] Strip / Pad foundation

C] Grillage foundation

D] Pile foundation

157] What is the name of foundation

A] Strip / Pad foundation

B] Stepped footing foundation

C] Strap foundation

D] Benching foundation

158] What is the name of foundation

A] Benching foundation

B] Strip / Pad foundation

C] Str / ap foundation

D] Pier foundation

159] Which pile anchor down the structure subjected to uplift due to hydrostatic pressure / over turning moment

A] Friction pile

B] End bearing pile

C] Tension pile D] Compaction pile

160] Which pile is used to protect water front structures against impact from ship / floating object

A] Batter pile

B] Fender piles

C] Tension pile

D] Anchor pile

161] Which foundation is preferred, if heavy inflow seepage and not possible to excavate the trenches and keep them dry

A] Raft foundation

B] Pile foundation
C] Grillage foundation
D] Cantilever foundation
162] What is the name of pile

A] Friction pile
B] Compaction pile
C] End learning pile
D] Batter pile
164] Which is the group of Raymond piles
A] Cased cast in situation concrete pile
B] Uncased cast in site pile
C] Precast concrete pile -
D] Non load bearing pile
165] What is the name of pile

A] Friction pile
B] Anchor pile
C] Compaction pile
D] End bearing pile
166] What is the name of pile

A] Friction pile

B] Under reamed pile

C] Anchor pile

D] Batter pile

167] Which pile provide secure against the horizontal pull from sheet piling

A] Friction pile

B] Tension pile

C] End bearing pile

D] Anchor pile

168] Which type of pile is termed as simplex pile

A] Cased cast in situation concrete pile

B] Uncased cast in situation concrete pile

C] Non load bearing pile

D] Timber pile

169] What is a temporary structure, to remove water and soil from an area and make it possible to carry out the construction work under reasonably dry condition , A] Cofferdam

B] Caisson

C] Pier foundation

D] Strip / Pad foundation

170] Which foundation is suitable, if no firm bearing strata exists at reasonable depth and the loading is uneven

A] Raft foundation

B] Grillage foundation

C] Combined footing foundation

D] Pile foundation

171] Which foundation is suitable, if the water table is very near to G.L and may defect the other types of form

A] Pile foundation

B] Raft foundation

C] Grillage foundation

D] Inverted arch foundation

172] Which piles are driven at angle to resist the large horizontal / inclined forces / A] Batter pile

B] Anchor pile

C] Uplift pile

D] Compaction pile

173] What is the name of foundation

A] Wall footing foundation

B] Combined footing foundation

C] Strip or Pad foundation

D] Strap footing foundation

174] What is the term that the horizontal members are parallel to the wall in scaffolding A] Putlog

B] Ledgers

C] Transome

D] Guard rail

175] What is the shoring

A] Raking shore

B] Single flying shore

C] Double flying shore

D] Dead or vertical shore

176] What is the shore having the distance between the parallel walls is 9 m to 12 m A] Raking shores

B] Single flying shores

C] Double flying shore

D] Dead or vertical shore

177] What is the scaffolding used for painting, pointing, while washing and maintenance work

A] Steel scaffolding

B] Trestle scaffolding

C] Cantilever scaffolding

D] Suspended scaffolding

178] What is the term generally used for the work such as arches and domes

A] Moulds

B] Stripping

C] Centering

D] Form work

179] What is the piling method carried out for trenches about 10 meters depth in soft grounds

A] Sheet piling

B] Stay bracing

C] Box sheeting

D] Vertical piling

180] What is the name of part marked as x

A] Ledger

B] Standard

C] Putlogs

D] Toe board

181] What is the name of part marked as x

A] Putlog

B] Standard

C] Braces

D] Transom

182] What is the distance between the (in single row) standards in single scaffolding A] 2.0 m

B] 1.7 m

C] 1.5 m

D] 1.2 m

183] What is the name of part marked as x

A] Jack

B] Bearing plate

C] Crib support

D] Needle beam

184] What is the name of part marked as x

A] Needle beam

B] Crib support

C] Bearing plate

D] Jack

185] What is the name of part marked as x

A] Crib support

B] Jack

C] Needle beam

D] Bearing plate

186] What is the depth of trench while box sheeting carried out in timbering in loose soil A] 4 m

B] 5 m

C] 5.5 m

D] 6 m

187] What is the name of part marked as x

A] Poling board

B] Wallings

C] Sheeting

D] Strut

188] What is the name of part marked as x

A] Sheetings

B] Strut

C] Wallings

D] Poling boards

189] What is the name of part marked as x

A] Temporary struts
B] Sheetings
C] Polling boards
D] Strut

190] What is the name of member that supports the boards in the centering of arches A] Turning piece
B] Props
C] Ribs
D] Laggings

191] What is the name of part marked as x

A] Boards
B] Prop
C] Turning piece
D] Arch

192] What is the name of part marked as x

A] Dead shore
B] Needle
C] Floor support

D] Braces

193] Which scaffold is suitable; if the construction work is to be carried out for upper floors A] Single scaffolding

B] Independent scaffolding

C] Suspended scaffolding

D] Needle scaffold

194] What is the name of scaffold, if it is formed with steel in special types of couplings and frames

A] Patented scaffold

B] Brick layers scaffold

C] Independent scaffold

D] Cantilever scaffold

195] What is the name of scaffold

A] Bricklayer scaffold

B] Cantilever scaffold

C] Independent scaffold

D] Double scaffolding

196] Which scaffold is suitable, if proper hard ground is not available for standards to rest A] Cantilever scaffold

B] Independent scaffold

C] Bricklayers scaffold

D] Suspended scaffold

197] What is the name of part marked as x

A] Ledgers

B] Cross brace

C] Standards

D] Diagonal brace

198] What is the name of timber piece used to give rigidity to frame work in timbering

A] Strut

B] Bracing

C] Sheeting

D] Poling boards

199] What is the approximate depth of vertical sheeting adopted in timbering in soft ground

A] 10m

B] 12m

C] 15m

D] 17m

200] What is the name of part marked as x

A] Poling board

B] Wallings

C] Strut

D] Sheeting

201] What is the name of part marked as x

A] Strut

B] Wallings

C] Poling board

D] Sheeting

202] What is the name of part marked as x

A] Sheeting

B] Wallings

C] Strut

D] Poling board

203] What is the minimum period for the removal of props to beams and arches for a span of 6m in centrering / form work

A] 10 Days

B] 14 Days

C] 17 Days

D] 20 Days

204] What is the name of part marked as x

A] Braces

B] Strut

C] Ribs

D] Ties

205] What is the name of part marked as x X

A] Ties
B] Centre block
C] Ribs
D] Strut

206] What is the name of part marked as x

A] Strut
B] Brace
C] Ribs
D] Lagging

207] What is the name of part marked as x

A] Laggings
B] Brace
C] Strut
D] Ribs

208] What is the name of part marked as x

A] Brace
B] Laggings
C] Ribs
D] Strut

209] What is the maximum suitable distance between the two adjacent parallel walls for single flying shore

A] 5 m

B] 9 m

C] 15 m

D] 18 m

210] Which shoreing is suitable, for existing foundations to be depended

A] Dead shore

B] Flying shore (Single)

C] Flying shore (Double)

D] Raking shore

211] What is the name of shore shown in elevation

A] Flying shore (Single)

B] Flying shore (Double)

C] Dead shore

D] Racking shore

212] What is the name of figure

A] Raking Shore

B] Flying shore (Single)

C] Flying shore (Double)

D] Dead shore

213] What is the name of part marked as x

A] Folding wedges
B] Cleat
C] Straining piece
D] Needle
214] Wh is the name of part marked as x

A] Sole plate
B] Hoop iron
C] Rakers
D] Wall plate
215] How to rectify if settlement of existing foundation has taken place
A] By timbering
B] Under pinning
C] Single scaffolding
D] Independent scaffolding
216] Which shoring is suitable, if the lower part of wall has become defective
A] Flying shore (Single)
B] Flying shore (Double)

C] Dead shore

D] Raking shore

217] What is the name of damp proofing method

A] Treatment to basement

B] Treatment to external walls

C] Treatment to sloping ground

D] Treatment to expansion joint in flat roof

218] What is the treatment to protect the building against termites to remove stumps, roots, logs and waste

A] Soil treatment

B] Structural treatment

C] Pre construction treatment

D] Post construction treatment

219] What is the structural member that should be constructed with fire resistant material and well separated from heat of the building

A] Wall openings

B] Floors and roofs

C] Walls and columns

D] Building fire escape element

220] What is the name of part marked as x

A] Lime concrete

B] DPC

C] Drip

D] RCC slab

221] What is the name of part marked as x

A] Brick jelly

B] Hot bitumen coating

C] Lime mortar

D] Mind puska

222] What is the material used for quick setting highly elastic and superior work

A] Barium plaster

B] Acoustic plaster

C] Gypsum plaster

D] Granite silicon plaster

223] Which plaster material is used for making the room sound proof

A] Burium B] Asbestos cement

C] Acoustic

D] Granite silicon

225] What is the common wall thickness for fire resistance

A] 45

B] 40

C] 30

D] 20

226] What is the defect in painting seen as glossy patches

A] Blistering

B] Flashing

C] Sagging

D] Fading

227] What is the defect in painting that loose small portion due to poor adhesion A] Flaking

B] Flashing

C] Blistering

D] Sagging

228] What is the stage of anti termite treatment done before laying the floor entire levelled surface s are treated at rate of 5 litre of emulsion/m2 -

A] Stage 1 1

B] Stage 2 2

C] Stage 3 3

D] Stage 4 4

229] What is the defect in formation of bubbles on painted surface due to water vapour A] Fading

B] Bloom

C] Blistering

D] Flashing

230] What is the part labelled as x

A] Crown

B] Extrados

C] Voussoirs

D] Outer curve of an arch

231] What is the name of arch having four centers

A] Elliptical

B] Venetian

C] Segmental

D] Equilateral pointed

232] What is the term for perpendicular distance between intrados and extrados

A] Kay

B] Pier

C] Rise

D] Depth

234] What is the name of the arch

A] Ogee arch
B] Tudor arch
C] Pointed arch
D] Florentine arch
235] What is the arch constructed over a wooden joist or flat arch
A] Stilted arch
B] Pointed arch
C] Relieving arch
D] Horse shoe arch
236] What is the lintel

A] Brick lintel
B] Steel lintel
C] Stone lintel
D] Reinforced cement concrete linte
237] What is the name of part marked as x

A] Key

B] Voussoirs
C] Extrados
D] Soffit
238] What is the name of the part marked as x The x

A] Soffit
B] Intrados
C] Extrados
D] Rise
239] Which arches is also called as lancet arches
A] Semi elliptical arches
B] Venetian elliptical arches
C] Relieving arches
D] Pointed arches
240] What is minimum range on wall provided for timber lintel bearing
A] 5 - 8 cm B] 8 - 13 cm
C] 15 - 20 cm
D] 25 - 30 cm
241] What is the centre to centre distance of stirrups at end in R.C.C Lintel
A] 10 cm
B] 15 cm
C] 18 cm
D] 22 cm
242] What is ratio of CC used in RCC lintel
A] 1]2]5
B] 1]2]4
C] 1]3]6
D] 1]4]6
243] What is the name of member, in centering of arches, a thick wooden plank shaped to the curvature of arch and it is supported by props
A] Ribs

B] Laggings C] Turning piece

D] Brace

244] How many centres are in tudor arches

A] 3

B] 4

C] 5

D] 6

245] What is the minimum period for the removal of props to beams for a span of 6 m in formwork

A] 15 Days

B] 17 Days

C] 21 Days

D] 25 Days

ANSWERS]

1]B ; 2]D; 3]A; 4]D; 5]C; 6]C; 7]B; 8]D; 9]B ; 10]B; 11]D; 12]C; 13]B; 14]D; 15]B; 16]A; 17]C; 18]B; 19]D; 20]C; 21]B; 22]D; 23]C; 24]B; 24a]D 25]D; 26]C; 27]B; 28]A; 28a]C 29]A; 30]C; 31]B; 32]D; 33]C; 34]B; 35]A; 36]C; 37]B; 38]D; 39]B; 40]A; 41]D; 42]B; 43]B; 44]A; 45]C; 46]A; 47]B; 48]D; 49]D; 49a]A; 50]C; 51]A; 52]D; 53]D; 54]C; 55]B; 56]A; 57]B; 58]C; 59]A; 60]A; 61]A; 62]C; 63]C; 64]B; 65]A; 66]C; 67]A; 68]C; 69]D; 70]C; 71]A; 72]B; 73]A; 73a]C; 74]B; 75]B; 76]A; 77]A; 78]D; 79]A; 80]D; 81]A; 82]A; 83]D; 84]D; 85]B; 86]B; 87]D; 88]B; 89]A; 90]B; 91]B; 92]B; 93]A; 94]C; 95]D; 96]B; 97]D; 98]A; 99]C; 100]D; 101]B; 102]C; 103]C; 104]B; 105]A; 106]D; 107]C; 108]A; 109]A; 110]A ; 111]C; 112]D; 113]A; 114]A; 115]B; 116]D; 117]A; 118]A; 119]B; 120]A; 121]A; 122]B; 123]C; 124]D; 125]B; 126]A; 127]C; 128]B; 129]A; 130]C; 131]A; 132]C; 133]D; 134]C; 135]D; 136]B; 137]A; 138]B; 139]D; 140]D; 141]A; 142]C; 143]A; 144]D; 145]A; 146]B; 147]C; 148]C; 149]D; 150]D; 151]D; 152]A; 153]C; 154]D; 155]A; 156]B; 156a]B; 157]D; 158]D; 159]C; 160]B; 161]B; 162]B; 163]C; 164]A; 165]D; 166]B; 167]D; 168]B; 169]A; 170]D; 171]A; 172]A; 173]C; 174]B; 175]B; 176]C; 177]D; 178]C; 179]A; 180]A; 181]B; 182]D; 183]A; 184]B; 185]C; 186]A; 187]C; 188]D; 189]A; 190]B; 191]C; 192]B; 193]D; 194]A; 195]B; 196]A; 197]D; 198]B; 199]A; 200]A; 201]B; 202]C; 203]B; 204]D; 205]B; 206]A; 207]B; 208]C; 209]B; 210]A; 211]C; 212]C; 213]A; 214]A; 215]B; 216]C; 217]B ; 218]C; 219]D; 220]B; 221]B; 222]D; 223]C; 224]B; 225]D; 226]B; 227]A; 228]C; 229]C; 230]A ; 231]B; 232]C; 233]B; 234]B; 235]C; 236]D; 237]A; 238]A; 239]D; 240]C; 241]C; 242]B; 243]C; 244]B; 245]C;

1] What is the work carried to fix national and state boundaries

A] Contouring

B] Levelling

C] Topographic mapping

D] Surveying

2] What is the length of one link in metric chain

A] 10 cm

B] 15 cm

C] 20 cm

D] 25 cm

3] What is the name of the setting out the work on the ground

A] Location survey

B] Preliminary survey

C] Topographical survey

D] Engineering survey

4] What is the principle of survey

A] Traverse

B] Triangulation

C] Work from whole to part

D] Work from part to whole

5] What is the method referred in chain surveying

A] Inter section method

B] Trilateration method

C] Triangular method

D] Polar co-ordinate method

6] What is the length of metric chain

A] 5m and 20m

B] 10m and 15m

C] 15m and 20m

D] 20m and 30m

7] What is the chain of 100 feet long generally used for taking offset in chain surveying 100 A] Gunter s chain

B] Revenue chain

C] Metric chain

D] Engineer s chain

8] What is the name of the equipment

A] Steel rod

B] Wooden peg

C] Off set rod

D] Ranging rod

9] What is the surface that is normal to the direction of gravity at all points

A] Levelling

B] Horizontal surface

C] Horizontal line

D] Level surface

10] What is the line that lies on a level surface and is normal to plumb line at all points A] Level line

B] Vertical line

C] Datum line

D] Horizontal line

11] What is the limit of error in 20m chain as per IS

A] ± 3 mm

B] ± 5 mm

C] ± 6 mm

D] ± 8 mm

12] What is the term for error that occur due to faulty adjustments of device such as chain may be too long or too short

A] Natural error

B] Personal error

C] Artificial error

D] Instrumental error

13] What is the limit of error for 30m chain as per IS 30m

A] ± 2 mm

B] ± 4 mm

C] ± 6 mm

D] ± 8 mm

14] Which type of tape is commonly used for measuring offset

A] Linen tape

B] Steel tape

C] Invar tape

D] Metallic tape

15] What is the error that arise due to variation of temperature

A] Natural error B] Personal error

C] Instrumental error

D] Artificial error

16] What is the length of metallic tape available in feet

A] 15 feet and 30 feet 15 30

B] 30 feet and 45 feet 30 45

C] 45 feet and 60 feet 45 60

D] 50 feet and 100 feet 50 100

17] What is the lateral surface distance measured from the chain to object

A] Off set

B] Long off set

C] Short off set

D] Oblique off set

18] What is the term that the distance measured at right angles to the chain line from the object

A] Short off set

B] Long off set

C] Oblique off set

D] Perpendicular off set

19] What is the offset that is measured other than right angle to the chain line from the object

A] Short off set

B] Long off set

C] Oblique off set

D] Perpendicular off set

20] What is the term that is normal to plumb line at all points

A] Level surface B] Datum surface

C] Horizontal surface

D] Vertical surface

21] What is the mark established between GTS bench marks by various government departments, PWD and other engineering agencies ,

A] Change point

B] Arbitrary bench mark

C] Permanent bench mark

D] Temporary bench mark

22] What is the bench mark established for short duration and the work should be resumed from these bench marks

A] G.T.S bench mark G.T.S

B] Arbitrary bench mark

C] Permanent bench mark

D] Temporary bench mark

23] How the chain is adjusted if the chain is found to increase in length than the standard length

A] By removing some of the rings

B] By straightening the bent of links

C] By adjusting the links at the handle

D] By inserting the new rings as required

24] What is thc lcngth if mctallic tapc available in meter

A] 5m and 10m

B] 10m and 15m

C] 15m and 20m

D] 15m and 30m

25] Which is location attraction in compass survey

A] Steel Structure

B] Building C] Trees

D] Hills

26] What is the direction of magnetic needle always pointing

A] East

B] West

C] South

D] North

27] What is the name of instrument

A] Pentagraph
B] Planimeter
C] Tachno meter
D] Speedo meter
28] What is the type of compass as per the system of graduation made

A] Magnetic compass
B] Trough compass
C] Prismatic compass
D] Surveyor s compass
29] Which method is used for plotting a traverse survey in compass

A] By included angle method
B] By paper protractor method

C] By Rectangle co-ordinate method

D] By graphical adjustment method

30] What is the error if the compass is affected by external influences

A] The pivot being bent

B] Local attraction

C] Inaccurate levelling

D] The vertical hair being thick

31] What is the error if the magnetic needle of a compass not being straight

A] Instrumental error

B] Manipulation error

C] Sighting error

D] External influences

32] Which method is more accurate in plotting a compass survey

A] Parallel meridian method

B] Included angle method

C] Paper protractor method

D] Rectangular co-ordinate method

33] What angle is differed due is local attraction at a particular place detected in fore and back bearing line

A] 45°

B] 90°

C] 180°

D] 270°

34] What is the true bearing, if the magnetic bearing of the line is N 37° W and the magnetic declination is 2°E ,

A] N 35° W

B] S 35° E

C] N 39° W

D] S 39° N

35] What is the variation of declination occured due to magnetic storms such as earth quakes and the amount of variation may be even 1° or 2°

A] Secular variation

B] Annual variation

C] Irregular variation

D] Regular Variation

36] What is the variation, in the magnetic merdian swings like a pendulum in one direction for a long period and gradually comes to rest and

then swings in the opposite direction A] Secular variation

B] Annual variation

C] Irregular variation

D] Daily variation

37] What is the compass with the graduations are marked as south with 0° and north with 180°

A] Trough compass

B] Magnetic compass

C] Surveyor compass

D] Prismatic compass

38] What is the direction indicated by an imaginary circle passing around the earth through the place north and south pole

A] True meridian

B] Arbitrary meridian

C] Magnetic meridian

D] Assured meridian

39] What is the compass that has graduation marked as 0° on North and South and 90° on Eastand West

A] Trough compass

B] Magnetic compass

C] Surveyor s compass

D] Prismatic compass

40] What is the sum of the interior angle of a pentagon

A] 260°

B] 360°

C] 440°

D] 540°

41] What is back bearing of AB if fore bearing of AB = 63° 30 AB = 63 ° 30

A] 243° 30 ‘

B] 116° 30’

C] 242° 30’

D] 115° 30’

42] What is the magnetic declination, if the magnetic bearing of the sun at noon is 354°

A] 5° W

B] 5° E

C] 6° E

D] 6° W

43b] What is back bearing of AB if fore bearing of
AB = N 32° 30’ E AB AB = N 32 ° 30
‘E AB

A] N 32° 30’ W

B] S 32° 30‘ W

C] N 32° 30’ S

D] S 32° 30‘ E

D] 67° 00’

43e] What is the true bearing, if the magnetic bearing of the line is N 37° W and the magnetic declination is 2°E

A] N 35° W

B] S 35° E

C] N 39° W

D] S 39° N

44] What is the name of the instrument

A] Clinometer

B] Abney level

C] Dumpy level

D] Telescopic alidade

45] What is the name of method in which tracing paper is used over the drawing sheet to solve the problems

A] Bessel s method

B] Traversing method

C] Trial and error method

D] Tracing paper method

46] What is name of the level which does not required any protection from the sun A] Auto level

B] Tilting level

C] Dumpy level

D] Wye (y) level

47] What is the name of the error that the fittings of table and tripod being loose A] Errors of manipulation

B] Errors of sighting

C] Errors of instrumental

D] Errors of plotting

48] How you will test the plane table board that the upper surface of the board should be perfect plane

A] Checks the straight edge in all directions

B] Set up and level the plane table over a station

C] If the bubble is not central position, the error by keeping packing between the underside of the board ,

D] Correct the edge by filling and again test

49] What is the colour of road metalled bridge

A] Burnt sienna

B] Burnt timber

C] Crimson Lake

D] Prussian blue

50] What is the term name for tracing the drawing by means of ink (inking) with order of tracing

A] Technique of tracing

B] Method of reproduction

C] Sequence of tracing

D] Should be traced in tracing cloth

51] What is the name of term that in this method of survey it is less costly than other types of survey

A] One of the advantages of plane table survey

B] One of the disadvantages of plane table survey

C] Survey can be done in dense wood areas

D] Great skill is required

52] What is name of the survey in which field work and plotting are done simultaneously in the field

A] Chain survey

B] Compass survey

C] Engineering survey

D] Plane table survey

53] What is the method of survey

A] Radiation

B] Resection

C] Traversing

D] Intersection

54] What is the method of survey

A] Radiation

B] Resection

C] Traversing

D] Intersection

55] What is the name of triangle formed by joining the ground points

A] Great triangle

B] Scalene triangle

C] Isosceles triangle

D] Equilateral triangle

56] What is the name of method

A] Two-point problem

B] Three-point problem

C] Tracing paper method

D] Graphical method

57] Which survey is most suitable for filling the various details between the stations fixed by triangulation

A] Levelling

B] Chain survey

C] Plane table survey

D] Compass survey

58] What is the method of survey

A] Radiation

B] Resection

C] Traversing

D] Intersecting

59] What is the name of method used in plane table survey similar to that of compass survey or theodolite

A] Radiation

B] Resection

C] Traversing

D] Intersection

60] What is the name of the process of putting the plane table with some fixed direction so that the line representing a particular direction on the plan is parallel to the direction on the ground

A] Centring the plane table

B] Orienting the plane table

C] Orienting by back sighting

D] Orienting by magnetic needle

61] What is the colour of compound walls

A] H - green -

B] Indigo

C] Burnt sienna

D] Burnt blue

62] Which place the plane table set up for prepare a road map

A] Centre of road

B] Left side of road

C] Right side of road

D] Along any one side of road

63] What is the colouring building benchmark

A] Burnt sienna

B] Burnt timber

C] Crimson lake

D] Prussian blue

64] What is the method with three known object points and its plotted position on the drawing sheet are taken for solving the problem

A] Lehman s rules

B] Mechanical method

C] Traversing method

D] Trial and error method

65] What is the name of problem

A] Two point problem

B] Three point problem

C] Bessel s method

D] Trial and error method

66] What is the name of method

A] Bessel s method

B] Two point problem

C] Mechanical method

D] Trial and error method

67] What is the method with any two of three known objects points and its plotted positions on the drawing sheet are taken for solving the problem

A] Lehman s rules

B] Bessel s method

C] Traversing method

D] Trial and error method

68] Which method of plane table survey the figure represents

A] Resection

B] Traversing

C] Radiation

D] Intersection

69] What is the name of level designated as self aligning level

A] Tilting level

B] Auto level

C] Dumpy level

D] Wye (Y) level

70] What is the name of the levelling instrument

A] Dumpy level
B] Wye (Y) level
C] Tilting level
D] Auto level
71] What is the name of the levelling instrument

A] Dumpy level
B] Wye (y) level C] Tilting level
D] Auto level
72] Which column is used, the first entry in the level book page
A] Fore sight
B] Back sight
C] Intermediate sight
D] Height of instrument
73] Which branch of surveying deals with the measurements in vertical plane
A] Chaining
B] Levelling
C] Compassing
D] Plane tabling
74] Which line is normal to plumb line at all points
A] Level line
B] Vertical line C] Curved line
D] Horizontal line

75] What bench mark is established for short duration such as at the end of a days work A] Arbitrary bench mark

B] Temporary bench mark

C] Permanent bench mark D] GTS bench mark

76] What is the name of the level that does not require any protection from the sun A] Titling level

B] Auto level

C] Dumpy level

D] Wye (y) level

77] What is the name of the staff used while the sights are long and the reading viewed through instrument

A] Solid staff

B] Invar staff

C] Target staff

D] Telescopic staff

78] What is the name of the staff 3m long and the band fitted is graduated in mm used for precise levelling

A] Solid staff

B] Invar staff

C] Folding staff

D] Telescopic staff

79] What is the smallest graduated division in levelling staff

A] 0.5 m

B] 0.05 m

C] 0.005 m

D] 0.0005 m

80] What is the figure describes

A] Reading the staff

B] Holding the staff

C] Adjusting the level

D] Levelling up the instrument

81] What is the message to indicate the movement of leftarm over 90°

90 °

A] Return to arm

B] Establish the position

C] Move my right

D] Move my left

82] What is the process if the difference of level between two points is determined by setting the levelling instrument midway between the point

A] Simple levelling

B] Profile levelling

C] Differential levelling

D] Reciprocal levelling

83] Which type of the collimation error is eliminated

A] Dumpy level

B] Wye (y) level

C] Cooke s reversible level

D] Cushing s level

84] What is the name of the imaginary line of constant elevation on the ground surface A] Relief

B] Contour line

C] Contouring line

D] Contour interval

85] What method of contour is suitable for small and low undulating area

A] By square method

B] By cross section method

C] By tachometry method

D] By levelling method

86] What method of contour is suitable for contouring in hilly areas

A] By square method

B] By cross section method

C] By tachometry method

D] By levelling method

87] What R.F is select the drawing of building sites as a topographic map

A] 1/100

B] 1/1000

C] 1/5000

D] 1/10000

88] What measurement are plotted to a plan or a map

A] Linear measurement

B] Angular measurement
C] Vertical measurement
D] Linear and angular measurement
89] What dimensions are drawn in a plan of contour
A] Vertical dimension
B] Horizontal dimension
C] Inclined dimension
D] Parallel dimension
90] What levelling is called as in direct levelling
A] Plane table levelling
B] Trigonometric levelling
C] Reciprocal levelling
D] Simple levelling
91] What will be the difference of level A and B if the B.S is 3.560m and F.S is 2.860m
A] 1.700 m
B] 1.600 m
C] 1.500 m
D] 0.700 m
92] What formula is used in arithmetic check in height of collimation method
A] B.S - F.S = Last R.L - First R.L
B] B.S + F.S = Last R.L - First R.L
C] B.S - F.S = last R.L - First R.L
D] B.S - F.S = Rise - Fan = Last R.L - First R.L
93] What is the height of collimation shown in figure with R.L 100.00 and B.S taken from A is 2.850 m

A] 100.520
B] 100.850
C] 102.850

D] 103.000

94] What is the purpose of using theodolite primarily

A] To measure vertical angle only

B] To measure inclined angle only

C] To measure horizontal angle only

D] To measure horizontal vertical angles

95] What is the instrument with its telescope can be revolved through 180° in a vertical plane about its horizontal axis

A] Auto level

B] Dumpy level

C] Transit theodolite

D] Non-Transit theodolite

96] What is the name of the part marked as X

A] Trivet

B] Eye piece

C] Telescope

D] Tripod head

97] What is the name of part marked as X

A] Level tube

B] Metal case

C] Bubble tube axis

D] Top of Telescopic axis

98] What is name of the component

A] Telescope
B] Dumpy level
C] Wye(Y) level
D] Cooke s level
99] What is referred to smallest measureable unit in theodolite
A] Double sighting
B] Least count
C] Swing
D] Contouring
100] What is the method in prolonging line?

A] Prolonging line by first method
B] Prolonging line by second method
C] Prolonging line by third method
D] Prolonging line by fourth method
101] What is the method of precisely the horizontal angle from a single station point can be measured
A] Reiteration method
B] Recipetation method
C] Radial method D] Off set method
102] What is the deflection angle that the angle measured in clockwise direction
A] Left deflection angle
B] Right deflection angle
C] Vertical deflection angle
D] Horizontal deflection angle
103] What is the name of theodolite with one of its telescope cannot be revolved through 180° in a vertical plane about its horizontal axis

A] Auto level
B] Dumpy level
C] Transit Theodolite
D] Non - Transit theodolite

104] what is the technical term for the process of bring the vertical axis of theodolite immediately over a mark or station point

A] Cantering
B] Traversing
C] Non - Traversing
D] Collimation

105] What is the term for rotating the telescope in horizontal plane about its vertical axis A] Cantering

B] Revolution
C] Swing
D] Sighting

106] Which method errors due to eccentricity of the spindles are eliminated by reading both the Vernier of the theodolite

A] Ordinary method
B] Repetition method
C] Recitation method
D] Compound method

107] What is the name of traversing that is used for running survey lines of a closed or open survey

A] Chain surveying
B] Compass surveying
C] Theodolite surveying
D] Plane table surveying

108] What is the method of prolongation of a straight line that result cumulative errors, if the instrument is not in adjustment

A] Prolonging a line by first method
B] Prolonging a line by second method
C] Prolonging a line by third method
D] Prolonging a line by fourth method

109] What is the method used for the instrument is suspected with improper adjustments and the error is doubled or reversal of telescope

A] Prolonging a line by 1st method
B] Prolonging a line by 2nd method
C] Prolonging a line by 3rd method

D] Prolonging a line by 4th method

110] What is the adjustment done to place the vertical axis exactly over the station A] Setting up

B] Centering

C] Levelling up

D] Focusing

111] Which method is adopted while the instrument in improper adjustment to establiish the intermediate point

A] Back sight

B] Fore sight

C] Single sighting

D] Double sighting

112] What is the test carried in theodolite to make the plate bubbles centre to run if the vertical axis is truly vertical

A] Spine test

B] Plate level

C] Collimation test

D] Bubble tube adjustment

113] What is the traversing that a device is used to fix direction

A] Chain traversing

B] Compass traversing

C] Theodolite traversing

D] Plane table traversing

114] What is the major disadvantage of open traverse

A] There is no check on summation of angles

B] Check both linear and angular measurement

C] Traverse are terminate at the same point

D] Mathematically closed and geometrically

115] What is the name of survey done after balancing traverse

A] Offset survey

B] Radial survey

C] Plotting a traverse survey

D] Bowditch s method

115a] What is the least count of theodolite instrument

A] 20’ 20"

B] 20‘ 10"

C] 0’ 20"

D] 20' 5"

115b] What is the one main scale division of vernier thedolite

A] 15' - 0"

B] 20' - 0"

C] 22' - 0"

D] 25' - 0"

116] What is the term referred as fixing of small timber battens to timber walls with laths and boards are nailed to it

A] Rebating

B] Studding

C] Mitering

D] Grooving

117] What is the maximum range of distance between vertical channels

A] 60 - 80 mm

B] 80 - 100 mm

C] 100 - 120 mm

D] 120 - 140 mm

118] What is the thumb rule for breadth of window

A] 1/5 (Width of room + Height of room)

B] 1/8 (Width of room + Height of room)

C] 1/10 (Width of room + Height of room)

D] 1/12 (Width of room + Height of room)

119] What is size of window shutter in window designation "12 WT 12" 12 WT 12

A] 1200 x 600 mm

B] 560 x 1100 mm

C] 1100 x 460 mm

D] 560 x 1200 mm

120] Which type of windows are controlled by pulling metal weight

A] Double Hung Pivoted Window

B] Casement Window

C] Bay Window

D] Clere storey Window

121] What is the ventilator provided in continuation of Door/Window at its top

A] Fanlight

B] Sky light

C] Dormer Window

D] Corner Window

122] Which window is provided on sloping roof

A] Table Window

B] Lantern Window

C] Dormer Window

D] Clerestory Window

123] What is the process of sinking the edge of one piece of timber to another by cutting grooves across its grains

A] Housing

B] Moulding

C] Planing

D] Chamfering

124] What is the name of carpentry joint

A] Matched and Beaded joint

B] Matched and V jointed joint

C] Dowelled joint

D] Ploughed and Tongued joint

125] What is the name of joint

A] Lapped joint
B] Fished joint
C] Scarfed joint
D] Tabled joint
126] What is the name of carpentry joints

A] Butt joint
B] Splayed joint
C] Rebated joint
D] Fished joint
127] What is the name of carpentry joint

A] Rebated and filleted joint
B] Rebated joint
C] Rebated Tongued and grooved joint
D] Tongued and grooved joint
128] What is the name of carpentry joint

A] Shouldered housed joint
B] Housed joint
C] Mitred rebated joint
D] Dovetailed housed joint
129] What is the name of carpentry joint

A] Angle halved joint
B] Tee-halved joint -
C] Dovetail halved joint
D] Bevel halved joint
130] What is the name of carpentry joint

A] Oblique - Tenon joint -
B] Birds mouth joint
C] Housed joint
D] Mitred and Rebated joint
131] What is the name of part marked as X

A] Bottom rail
B] Top rail
C] Lock rail
D] Frame

132] What is the name of part marked as X

A] Hold fast
B] Horn
C] Frame
D] Style

133] Which is used to subdivide a door or window with a vertical member of a frame A] Mullion
B] Transom
C] Style
D] Lock rail

134] What is a depression / recess inside the doorframe to receive the shutter

A] Mullion
B] Transom
C] Rebate
D] Sill

135] What is the relationship of width of door and H height of door

A] H = (Width + 1.5 m) H = (+ 1.5)
B] H = (Width + 1.35 m) H = (+ 1.35)
C] H = (Width + 1.2 m) H = (+ 1.2)
D] H = (Width + 1.1 m) H = (+ 1.1)
136] What is the name of part marked as X

A] Lipping
B] Batten core
C] Cross band
D] Panel
137] What is the name of hinge

A] Counter flap hinge
B] Butt hinge
C] Back flap hinge
D] Garnet flap hinge
138] What is the size of opening for designation “6 WS 12” "6 WS 12"
A] 600 x 1200
B] 1200 x 1000
C] 1200 x 1200
D] 1000 x 1000
139] Which window is provided near the top of main roof
A] Panelled Window
B] Casement Window

C] Clere storey Window
D] Table Window
140] What is the road safety Sign

A] Mandatory sign
B] Cautionary sign
C] Informatory sign
D] Prohibition sign
141] What is the name of tool

A] Wire Stripper
B] Crimping tool
C] Combination pliers
D] Diagonal cutting piers
142] What is the unit of electrical resistance
A] Volt
B] Ohm
C] Watt
D] Ampere
143] Which instrument is used to measure electric current
A] Ammeter
B] Voltmeter
C] Wattmeter
D] Ohm meter
144] How many electrons are there in the third shell of copper atom
A] 8
B] 13
C] 18 D] 29
145] Which is a conductor of electricity
A] Mica
B] Copper
C] Air

D] Glass

146] Which is a temporary wiring

A] Casing and capping wiring

B] CTS/TRS wiring C] Cleat wiring

D] Lead sheathed wiring

147] What is the name of diagram

A] Layout diagram

B] Installation diagram

C] Circuit diagram

D] Wiring diagram

148] What is the unit for quantity of electricity

A] Mho

B] Coloumb

C] Volt/Second

D] Ampere/Second

149] What is the first aid to be given to stop the bleeding of the victim

A] Applying ointment

B] Keep the injured portion upward

C] Covering the wound portion by dressing

D] Applying pressure over the injured portion

150] What is the golden hour for victim injured on head with risk of dying

A] First 15 minutes

B] First 30 minutes

C] First 45 minutes

D] First 60 minutes

151] Which condition of the victim is referred as COMA stage

A] Unconscious but can respond to calls

B] unconscious but cannot respond to calls

C] Breathing but cannot respond to calls

D] Lie totally senseless and do not respond to call

152] What is the use of tool

A] Holding the hot substances

B] Calling and twisting wires

C] Extracting nails from wood

D] Loosening and tightening of bolls and nuts

153] What is the purpose of switch in electrical circuit

A] Regulate the rated supply voltage

B] control the amount of current through load

C] Start (or) stop the flow of current

D] Provide the path for the current to flow

154] What is the indication of neon polarity indicator used for checking AC supply AC A] Both electrodes will glow

B] Only one electrode will glow

C] Both electrodes will be flickering

D] One electrode will glow and another will be flickering

155] Which instrument is used to test the new wiring installation

A] Multimeter

B] Ohmmeter

C] Voltmeter

D] Megger

156] What effect of electric current is applied in ceiling fan

A] Heating effect

B] Chemical effect

C] Magnetic effect

D] Gas ionization effect

157] What is the maximum permissible load for a light and fan sub circuit as per IE rules

A] 800 watt

B] 1500 watt

C] 2000 watt

D] 3000 watt

158] Which is the polarity of direct current (DC)

A] Phase (L) and Neutral (N)

B] Phase (L) and Negative (-ve)

C] Positive (+ve) and Neutral (N)

D] Postive (+ve) and negative (-ve)

158a] What immediate action to be taken if a person get electric shock

A] Report to your authority

B] Call for the doctor for medical treatment

C] Call other persons for help to rescue true victim

D] Switch 'OFF' the power supply

159] What is the name of floor

A] Marble floor

B] Muram floor

C] Mosaic floor

D] Solid ground floor

160] What is the span for provision of herringbone strutting in single joist timber floor A] 1.0

B] 1.5 m

C] 2.0 m

D] 2.4 m

161] What is the maximum span for single joist timber floor

A] 2.5 m

B] 3.0 m

C] 3.6 m

D] 4.0 m

162] What is the name of part marked as X

A] Ceiling joist
B] Wall plate
C] Common rafter
D] Herring Bone strutting
163] What is the intermediate support in timber framed floor
A] Joist
B] Binders
C] Common rafter
D] Strutting
164] What is the name of part marked as X

A] Strutting
B] Furring piece
C] Air space
D] Binders
165] What is the rise range in Jack floor
A] 25 to 30 cm
B] 20 to 25 cm
C] 10 to 20 cm D] 30 to 35 cm
166] Which floor is applied with a thin coat of cement-cow-dung --
A] Murum Floor
B] Linoleum Floor
C] Mud Floor
D] Asphalt Floor
167] Which is a form of disintegrated rock with building material
A] Flagstone
B] Murum
C] Mosaic
D] Granolithic
168] What is the ratio of cement mortar for pointing in flagstone laying
A] 1]2
B] 1]3
C] 1]4
D] 1]5
169] Which floor is resilient and noise proof

A] Asphalt floor

B] Cement concrete floor

C] Rubber floor

D] PVC floor

170] What is the name of part marked as x

A] Wall plate

B] Bridging joist

C] Common rafter

D] Floor boards

171] Which system of reinforcement is preferred in R.C.C upper floor for ordinary loading condition

A] One way

B] 4 way

C] 2 way

D] Combined 2 and 4 way

172] Which floor is convenient to carryout plumbing and electrical installation without affecting the appearance

A] Rib floor

B] R.C.C floor

C] Timber floor

D] Jack arch floor

173] Which floor do not require form work during construction

A] Precast concrete floor

B] Double flange stone floor

C] Jack arch floor

D] Filler joist floor

174] What is the name of layer marked as x

A] Compacted earth filling

B] Sand filling

C] Lean

D] Cement concrete

175] What is the thickness of plain cement concrete laid for the brick floor

A] 5 - 7.5 cm

B] 10 - 15 cm

C] 16 - 20 cm

D] 21 - 25 cm

176] What is the proportion of lean cement concrete used in cement concrete floor

A] 1]1]2

B] 1]1½] 3

C] 1]2]4

D] 1]3]6

177] Which floor wax is applied as a final coat of polishing to get glossy surface A] Mosaic floor

B] Terrazzo floor

C] Flagstone floor

D] Granolithic floor

178] Which floor with a concrete base is spread and levelled with 5 to 8 cm thick lime-surkhi mortar

A] Terrazzo floor

B] Granolithic floor

C] Mosaic floor

D] Flagstone

179] Which floor is used for surface subjected to heavy wear like dairies and hospital A] Granolithic floor

B] Asphalt floor

C] Terrazzo floor

D] Cement concrete floor

180] What is the ratio of cement mortar used to fix tiles on floor

A] 1] 2

B] 1] 1

C] 1] 3

D] 1] 4

181] Which floor is constructed with cement concrete 1]1]3 and aggregates used are limestone, quartz silt and ballast

A] Mosaic

B] Granolithic Granolithic C] Marble

D] Cement concrete

182] What is the name of part marked as x

A] Baffile Baffile

B] Curtain wall

C] Main wall

D] Sleeper wall

183] Which vertical transportation is suitable for large number of people

A] Stairs B] Ramp

C] Escalator

D] Lift

184] What is the range of angle for stair

A] 40° to 45° 40 ° 45 °

B] 45° to 60° 45 ° 60 ° C] 25° to 30° 25 ° 30 °

D] 30° to 40° 30 ° 40 °

185] What is the name of part marked as x

A] Going
B] Baluster
C] Handrail
D] Newel post
186] What is one end or both ends corners cut in plan of a step
A] Commode
B] Splayed
C] Bull nose
D] Dancing step
187] What is the name of part marked as x

A] Tread
B] Going
C] Nosing
D] Scotia
188] What is the name of part marked as x

A] Tread
B] Riser
C] Stringer
D] Going
189] What is the combined framework of handrail and baluster in a stair

A] Barrister B] Stair

C] Landing

D] Stringer

190] What is an ordinary step of rectangular shape in plan

A] Flier

B] Going

C] Tread

D] Riser

191] Which type of stair with the steps are radiated from one point to upper floor A] Geometrical stair

B] Helical stair

C] Half turn stair

D] Three quarter turn stair

192] What is a stair turning through one right angle

A] Quarter turn stair

B] Half turn stair

C] Three quarter stair

D] Geomatrical stair

193] What is a stair branched in two flights at building

A] Geometrical stair

B] Bifurcated stair

C] Dog legged stair

D] Open Newel stair

194] What is a stair if its flights run opposite direction and there is no space between the flights ,

A] Open Newel stair

B] Geometrical stair

C] Three-quarter turn stair -

D] Doglegged stair

195] What is the name of stair

A] Geometrical stair

B] Half turn stair
C] Circular stair
D] Quarter turn stair
196] What is the name of stair

A] Three quarter turn stair
B] Half turn stair
C] Quarter turn stair
D] Biffurcated stair
197] What is the name of stair

A] Circular stair
B] Bifurcated stair
C] Geometrical stair
D] Doglegged stair
198] What is the inclination of Escalator
A] 45°
B] 40°
C] 35°
D] 30°
199] What is the name of stone step

A] Cantilever step
B] Spandril step
C] Built up step
D] Tread and riser step
200] What is the name of stone step

A] Rectangular step
B] Spandril step
C] Cantilever step
D] Cantilever tread and riser step
201] What is the minimum width of a stair
A] 70 cm
B] 80 cm
C] 90 cm
D] 100 cm
202] What is the stairs flight having an opening between two flights
A] Half turn stair
B] Geometrical stair
C] Open Newel stair
D] Three quarter turn stair
203] What is the minimum thickness range of stringer used in wooden stair
A] 30 to 50 mm
B] 50 to 70 mm
C] 70 to 80 mm
D] 80 to 90 mm

.

204] What is the Height of riser in a stair

A] riser of Numberfloor of Height Total

B] (Number of riser - 1)

C] (Number of riser - 2)

D] Number of riser - 3

205] What is the number of steps required if the Height of floor is 3.0 m assume the rise is 15 cm for a single flight

A] 21

B] 20

C] 19

D] 18

206] What is the number of treads if the height of floor is 3.8 m and assume rise is 14 cm for double flight

A] 23

B] 24

C] 25

D] 26

Draughtsman Civil – Semester 2 Module 10] Roof and Roof Covering

207] Which rafter support extend from eaves to ridge

A] Valley rafter

B] Ridge rafter

C] Common rafter

D] Principle rafter

208] What is a rafter provided at junction of two slopes

A] Jack rafter

B] Common rafter

C] Hip rafter

D] Principle rafter

209] What is the edge of roof running between the eaves and ridge

A] Verge

B] Cleat

C] Template

D] Purlin

210] What is the name of part marked as X

A] Hip
B] Fascia board
C] Eaves
D] Soffit
211] What is the name of part marked as X

A] Dormer
B] Fascia
C] Stepped flashing
D] Soffit
212] What is the name of part marked as X

A] Hip
B] Valley
C] Ridge
D] Wall plate
213] What is termed as the inclination of roof
A] Eaves
B] Pitch
C] Hip

D] Gable
214] What is theame of roof

A] Hip roof
B] Gable roof
C] Gambrel roof
D] Mansard roof
215] What is the name of part marked as X

A] Corbel
B] Corvice
C] Blocking stone
D] Wall plate
216] What is the economical span for collar beam roof
A] 5.5 m
B] 5.0 m
C] 4.7 m
D] 4.3 m
217] What is the name of part marked as X

A] Cleat
B] Battens
C] Purlin
D] Common ratfer
218] What is the name of part marked as X

A] King post
B] Strut
C] Purlin
D] Principal rafter
219] What is the economical span range for the king post truss
A] 5 to 8 m
B] 3 to 4.5 m
C] 9 to 10 m
D] 11 to 12 m
220] What is the name of part marked as X

A] Straining beam
B] Tie rod
C] Collar
D] Strut
221] What is the name of part marked as X

A] Valley beam
B] Edge beam
C] Tie beam
D] Intermidiate beam
222] What is the name of roof

A] Barrel vault shell roof
B] Bowstring steel roof
C] Steel frame dome
D] Belfast roof
223] What is the name of roof

A] Truncated roof
B] Belfast roof
C] North light roof
D] Bowstring steel roof
224] What is the brick size used in Madras terrace roof
A] 10 x 60 x 20 cms
B] 12 x 65 x 20 cms
C] 18 x 80 x 25 cms

D] 15 x 75 x 25 cms

226] Which flat roof is provided with tie rod

A] R.C.C floor

B] Bengal terrace

C] Madras terrace

D] Jack arch floor

227] How many days are recommended to set the concrete generally in Madras Terrace roof A] 2

B] 3

C] 4

D] 5

228] How much surface slope is provided in Bengal Terrace roof

A] 5 to 7 cm

B] 8 to 10 cm

C] 13 to 15 cm

D] 18 to 20 cm

229] What is the Brick Bat concrete thickness generally adopted for Madras terrace roof A] 125 mm

B] 100 mm

C] 75 mm

D] 60 mm

230] What is the centre-to-centre distance of joist in Brick concrete terrace roof --

A] 30 cm

B] 15 cm

C] 60 cm

D] 75 cm

231] What is the name of part marked as X

A] Collar

B] Tie beam

C] Straining beam

D] Straining sill

232] What is the name of roof

A] Mansard roof
B] Deck roof
C] Gambrel roof
D] Gable roof
233] What is the name of roof

A] Mansard roof
B] Gambrel roof
C] Hipped roof
D] Gabled roof
234] What is the name of part marked as X

A] Collar
B] Purlin
C] Tie beam
D] Wall plate
235] Which truss consists of wooden member and steel or wrought iron member
A] Truncated truss
B] Composite truss
C] Compound truss
D] King and queen post truss
236] Which truss consists of thin timber section at its top chord curved

A] Truncated truss
B] Bow string truss
C] Bel fast truss
D] Mansard roof truss
237] Name the roof truss

A] North light roof truss
B] Simple fink truss
C] Compound fink truss
D] House steel truss
238] What is the maximum slope given to the flat roof
A] 5°
B] 6°
C] 8°
D] 10°
239] Which roof is useful that is provided on circular brick
A] Barrel vault shell roof B] Steel frame dome
C] Belfast roof
D] Bowstring roof
240] What is the name of part marked as X

A] Lime concrete filling
B] Cement concrete filling
C] Sand filling
D] Earth filling
241] What is the slope usually given on R.C.C flat roof

A] 1 in 15
B] 1 in 20
C] 1 in 60
D] 1 in 130

242] What is the centre-to-centre distance of battens in Bengal Terrace roof

A] 15 cm B] 20 cm.
C] 25 cm
D] 30 cm

243] What is the centre-to-centre distance of rafters in Bengal Terrace roof

A] 20 cm
B] 30 cm
C] 40 cm
D] 50 cm

ANSWERS]

1]D ; 2]C; 3]A; 4]C; 5]D; 6]D; 7]D; 8]C; 9]D; 10]A; 11]B; 12]D; 13]D; 14]D; 15]A; 16]D; 17]A; 18]D; 19]C; 20]B; 21]C; 22]D; 23]A; 24]D; 25]A; 26]D; 27]B; 28]C; 29]A; 30]B; 31]C; 32]D; 33]C; 34]A; 35]C; 36]A; 37]D; 38]A; 39]C; 40]D; 41]A; 42]C; 43]C; 43a]B; 43b]B; 43c]C; 43d]A; 43e]A; 44]D; 45]D; 46]A; 47]C; 48]A; 49]A; 50]A; 51]A; 52]D; 53]B; 54]C; 55]A; 56]A; 57]C; 58]D; 59]C; 60]B; 61]B; 62]D; 63]C; 64]B; 65]B; 66]D; 67]B; 68]C; 69]B; 70]A; 71]D; 72]B; 73]B; 74]D; 75]B; 76]B; 77]D; 78]B; 79]C; 80]B; 81]C; 82]A; 83]C; 84]B; 85]A; 86]C; 87]B; 88]D; 89]B; 90]B; 91]D; 92]A; 93]C; 94]C; 95]C; 96]B; 97]C; 98]A; 99]B; 100]C; 101]A; 102]B; 103]D; 104]A; 105]C; 106]A; 107]C; 108]A; 109]C; 110]B; 111]D; 112]B; 113]B; 114]A; 115]C; 115a]C; 115b]B; 116]B; 117]C; 118]B; 119]B; 120]A; 121]A; 122]C; 123]A; 124]B; 125]A; 126]B; 127]C; 128]D; 129]B; 130]A; 131]C; 132]A; 133]A; 134]C; 135]C; 136]B; 137]D; 138]A; 139]C; 140]A; 141]C; 142]B; 143]A; 144]C; 145]B; 146]C; 147]A; 148]B; 149]D; 150]B; 151]D; 152]C; 153]C; 154]A; 155]D; 156]C; 157]A; 158]D; 158a]D; 159]D; 160]D; 161]C; 162]D; 163]B; 164]B; 165]C; 166]C; 167]B; 168]B; 169]C; 170]A; 171]C; 172]A; 173]A; 174]D; 175]B; 176]D; 177]B; 178]C; 179]B; 180]B; 181]B; 182]D; 183]B; 184]D; 185]D; 186]B; 187]D; 188]C; 189]A; 190]A; 191]B; 192]A; 193]B; 194]D; 195]B; 196]A; 197]C; 198]D; 199]D; 200]B; 201]B; 202]C; 203]A; 204]A; 205]C; 206]A; 207]C; 208]C; 209]A; 210]B; 211]C; 212]C; 213]B; 214]B; 215]A; 216]B; 217]B; 218]D; 219]A; 220]B; 221]A; 222]C; 223]C; 224]D; 225]D; 226]D; 227]B; 228]C; 229]C;

230]A; 231]A; 232]B; 233]A; 234]A; 235]B; 236]C; 237]A; 238]D; 239]A; 240]A; 241]C; 242]A; 243]B;

www.ingramcontent.com/pod-product-compliance
Ingram Content Group UK Ltd.
Pitfield, Milton Keynes, MK11 3LW, UK
UKHW021915190726
13853UKWH00002B/683

9 798888 055878